The Billionare's Club: The Top 25 Federal Contractors

Introduction

Thank you purchasing **The Billionaire's Club: The Top 25 Federal Contractors**. The information you are about to delve into will provide you with Companies who during 2012 into Mid- 2013 are the Top 25 Contractors with the Federal Government. As you would expect we cannot guarantee that all of this information is 100 per cent correct. It was collected from USAGOV, GAO, GSA and other sources on the Internet. It is however as accurate as we can make it.

For the Small Business reader we have included a copy and URL to each of the Companies (if they had one) so you could register and begin to explore possible relationships with these very successful firms.

The Table of Contents is active, since sometimes when you format a Kindle book the pages numbers get thrown out. So all you need to do is **Click on the Company you wish to look for....**

The Whetzel Group, Inc. will continue to bring you the latest information on the Government Sector. We specialize in support to Small Businesses through our online training, and training video's

You can visit us at the following Website:
www.whetzelgroup.com.

    We hope you enjoy this book; and of course we are always looking for ways to improve our products. If you have any comments or suggestions please email us at info@whetzelgroup.com,

    Once again thank you for purchasing our Product.

Howard C. Whetzel

Howard C. Whetzel
President/CEO
The Whetzel Group, Inc.

TABLE OF CONTENTS

1: Lockheed Martin Corp.	5
To become a potential Lockheed Martin supplier, please register by following these	6
2: Northrop Grumman Corp.	7
NGC Supplier Registration:	8
3: Boeing Co.	9
Introduce Your Company to Boeing	10
4: Raytheon Co.	11
Raytheon Supplier Diversity	12
Raytheon Supplier Registration:	12
5: Science Applications International Corp. (SAIC)	13
Submit Profile	14
6: General Dynamics Corp.	15
General Dynamics	16
7: Hewlett---Packard Co./EDS	18
HP Enterprise Services Business Information Request:	18
8: Booz Allen Hamilton Inc.	19
Doing Business with Booz Allen Hamilton	20
BAH Business Registration Portal:	20
9. Computer Science Corporation	22
CSC Supplier Registration:	22
10: L---3 Communications Inc.	23
SUPPLIER REGISTRATION	24
11: DynCorp International LLC	25
Partners in Innovation	26
supply@dyn---intl.com	26
12: CACI International Inc.	27
Becoming a Supplier	31
Prospective Supplier Form:	
13 Harris Corporation	31
14: Verizon Communications Inc.	32
15: ManTech International Corp.	34
Supplier Outreach	35
16: Fluor Corp.	36
Suppliers	37
17: AT&T Inc.	38
Supplier Information	39
NOTE:	39
18: BAE Systems	40
Suppliers	41
19: Dell Computer Corp.	42
20: United Technologies Corp.	44
21: IBM Corp.	46
22: Exelis (formally ITT)	48
Suppliers	
23: Jacobs Engineering Group	49
24: Deloitte	55
25: Accenture Ltd	57
Accenture Supplier Registration:	58

4

1: Lockheed Martin Corp.

Top 100 Revenue:

$14,947,961,000

Headquarters:

Bethesda Md.

Web address: http://www.lockheedmartin.com
President/CEO: Marillyn A. Hewson, president and CEO

Head of gov't business: Sondra L. Barbour, executive vice president, information systems and global services

Ticker: LMT

Lines of business: Aeronautics, electronic systems, information systems and global services and space systems

Major customers: Defense Department, Nuclear Regulatory Commission, Federal Aviation Administration, NASA, National Security Agency, Census Bureau, Energy Department and National Oceanic and Atmospheric Administration

Major contracts/projects: Lockheed Martin is providing integrated site-wide services to the Energy Department and other contractors at the Hanford site in south central Washington State. The Mission Support contract is worth $3 billion over 10 years.

To become a potential Lockheed Martin supplier, please register by following these instructions:

1.) Go to Exostar
2.) Select LM P2P Unsolicited Registration Request
3.) Complete the form
4.) If you would like to share additional information about your firm, send an e-mail containing a brief description of your firm's capabilities, business size and status to supplier.communications@lmco.com.

If you need assistance with Exostar, call: 703-*793*-7800

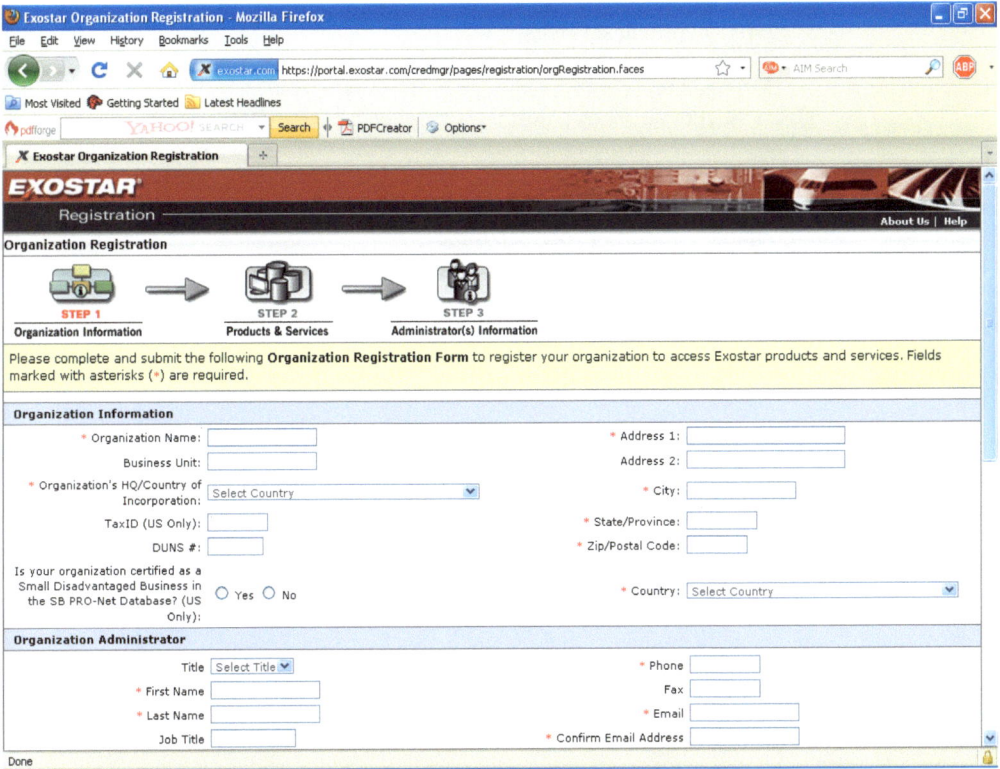

2: Northrop Grumman Corp.

Top 100 Revenue: $8,566,522,000

Headquarters: Los Angeles/Falls Church

Web address: http://www.northropgrumman.com

President/CEO: Wes Bush, chairman and CEO

Head of gov't business: Sid Ashworth, corporate vice president and president, Northrop Grumman Information Systems

Ticker: NOC

Lines of business: Aerospace systems, information systems, shipbuilding, electronic systems, technical services

Major customers: Defense Department, Centers for Disease Control, U.S. Coast Guard and Homeland Security

Major contracts/projects: Northrop Grumman is providing IT services and associated enabling products to the military, Defense Department and other agencies under the $12.2 billion ENCORE II contract.

NGC Supplier Registration:
https://oasis.northgrum.com

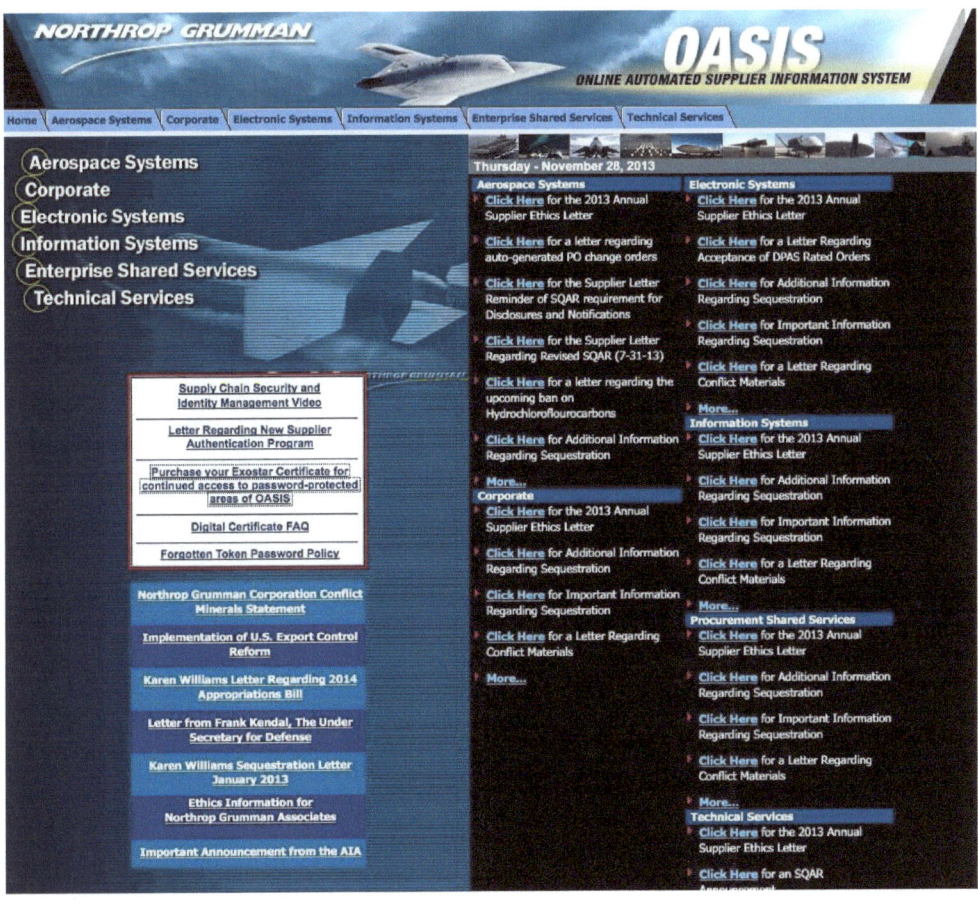

3: Boeing Co.

Top 100 Revenue: $7,131,867,000

Headquarters:	Chicago
Web address:	http://www.boeing.com
President CEO	W. James McNerney Jr., chairman, president and CEO
Head of gov't business:	Dennis A. Mullenburg, president and CEO, Boeing Defense, Space and Security
Ticker:	BA
Lines of business:	Commercial airplanes, defense, space and security, Boeing Capital Corp., and shared services group
Major customers:	NASA, Defense Department and Homeland Security Department
Major contracts/projects:	Boeing is the prime contractor on the multi-billion dollar SBInet project to build a virtual fence on the Mexican-U.S. border. Boeing also is under contract to build 12 GPS IIF satellites for the military's satellite-based radio navigation system that permits land, sea and airborne users to instantaneously and precisely determine their three-dimensional position, velocity and time.

Introduce Your Company to Boeing

If you are a small and/or diverse company interested in doing business with Boeing, we Suggest the following steps to introduce your company to us.

- Enter your company profile into the U.S. Government's Central Contractor Registration (CCR) database, now know as SAM. The SAM incorporates the former PRO-Net, the SBA's online database of small, small disadvantaged and woman-owned, HubZone, and veteran-owned businesses wanting to do business with the federal government or its prime contractors.
- Boeing Supplier Introduction process: Register your company in our Boeing Supplier GATEWAY database by completing the online Supplier GATEWAY profile with details of your company and what it has to offer. This database is used by Boeing Supplier Management, Engineering and other organizations to search for suppliers whose capabilities match potential bid opportunities.

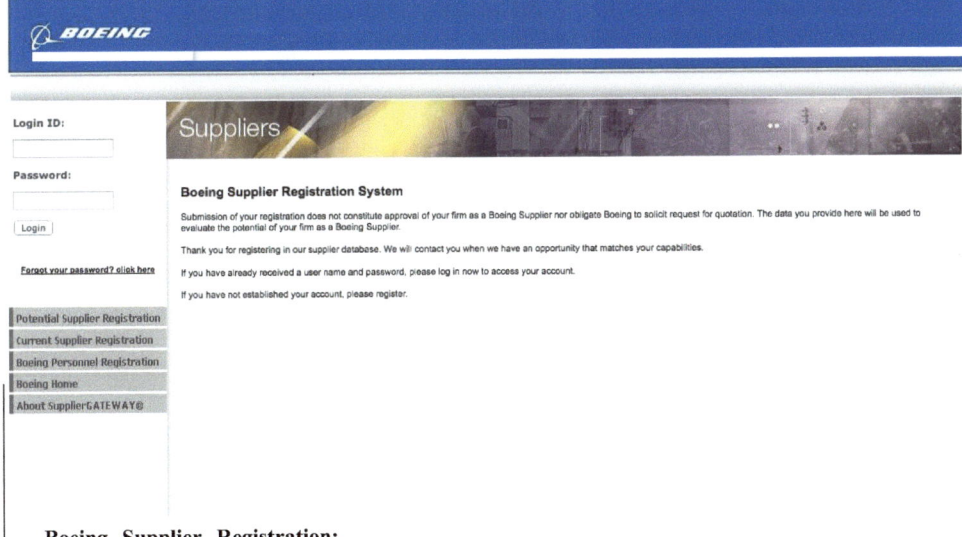

Boeing Supplier Registration:
https://app.suppliergateway.com/boeing/Login.as

4: Raytheon

Revenue: $6,110,641,000

Headquarters:	Waltham, MA
Web address:	http://www.raytheon.com
President/CEO:	William H. Swanson, chairman and CEO
Head of gov't business:	Daniel L. Smith, president, integrated defense systems
Ticker:	RTN
Lines of business:	Integrated defense systems, intelligence and information systems, missile systems, network centric systems, Raytheon Technical Services Company LLC and space and airborne systems
Major customers:	U.S. Missile Defense Agency, NASA, Army, Navy, Marine Corps, Air Force and Homeland Security Department
Major contracts/projects:	Raytheon was hired by NASA on a subcontract for systems engineering and design, Web development and information technology services to support the Jet Propulsion Laboratory's mission. The contract is worth $83 million.

Raytheon Supplier Diversity

"We are building an inclusive culture"

Raytheon's Supplier Diversity Program strives to provide an inclusive environment to do business with small, minority-owned, women-owned, veteran-owned (including service disabled veterans), and HubZone businesses.

Raytheon also seeks to provide an inclusive environment for historically black colleges, universities, and minority institutions to participate in the procurement of technical, engineering, and research services.

To that end, Raytheon is committed to a diverse supply base that reflects the demographics and values of our Company, customers, and the communities in which we operate.

Raytheon Supplier Registration:
http://www.raytheon.com/connections/supplier/registration/index.html

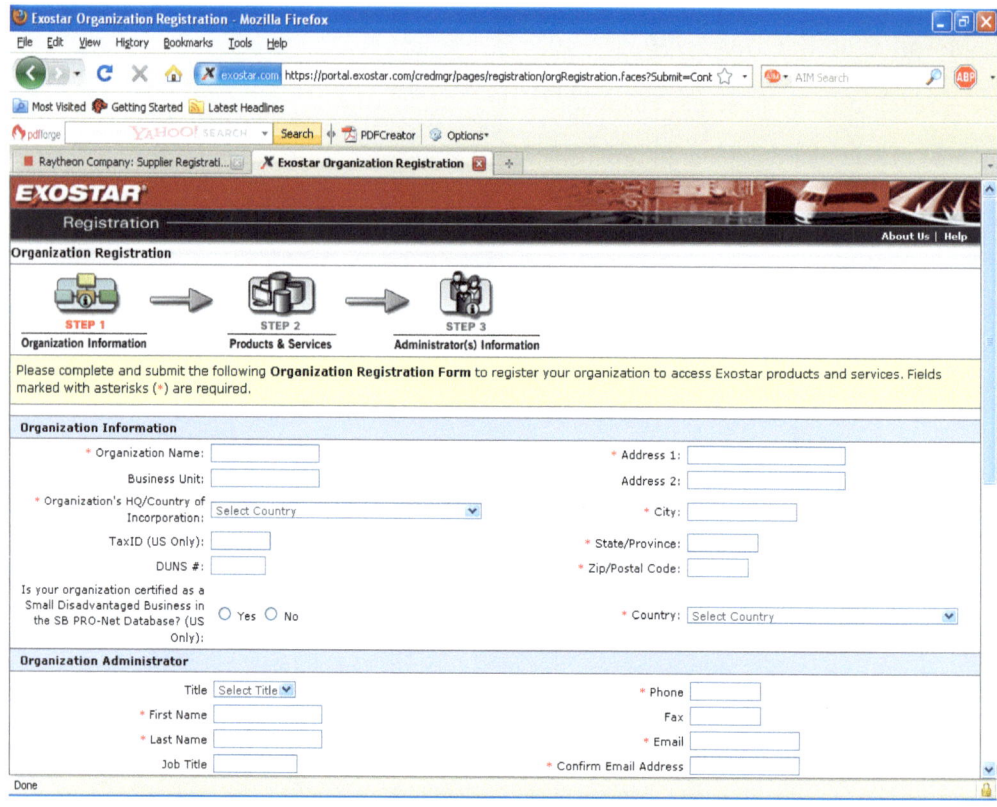

5: Science Applications International Corp. (SAIC)

Revenue: $5,988,489,000

Headquarters: McLean, VA

Web address: http://www.saic.com
President/CEO: Walter P. Havenstein, CEO
Head of gov't business: Charles F. Koontz, president, information technology and network solutions group
Ticker: SAI

Lines of business: Defense Department, Health Care Systems Integration, Intelligence Community

Major contracts/projects: SAIC has a task order by the Defense Health Information Management System to provide sustainment support to the Armed Forces Health Longitudinal Technology Application Composite Health Care System. The work is worth more than $158 million.

SAIC split into SAIC and LEIDOS Inc. in 2013 You can sign up for LEIDOS at www.leidos.com

https://contacts.leidos.com/sPortal/suppass.nsf/LandingPage?OpenForm

Submit Profile

Submit your company profile to be considered for future teaming opportunities with SAIC. SAIC program managers, business developers, and contracts and procurement personnel access this information actively to identify capable small businesses for teaming opportunities on current and upcoming programs.

SAIC Supplier Form:
http://contacts.saic.com/sbsExt.nsf/extSubmit?OpenForm

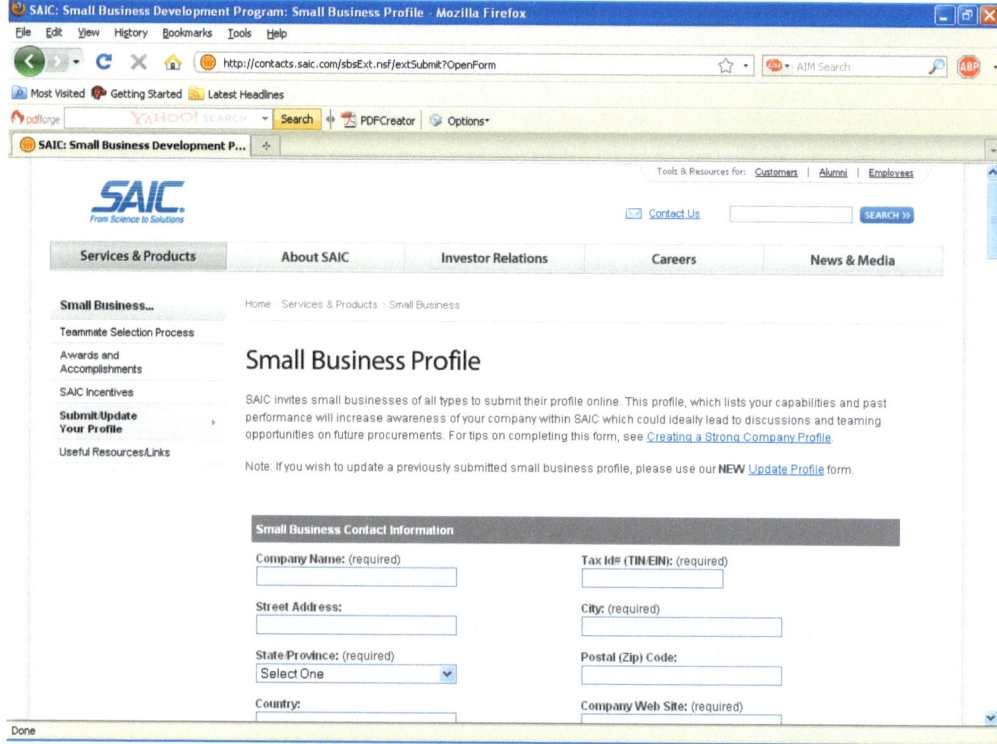

6: General Dynamics Corp.

Revenue: $4,658,261,000

Headquarters: Falls Church, VA

Web address: http://www.gd.com

Chairman/CEO: Phebe N. Novakovic,

Head of gov't business: David K Heebner, executive vice president, information systems and technology

Ticker: GD

Lines of business: Aerospace, combat systems, marine systems and information systems and technology

Major customers: Defense Department, U.S. armed forces, Health and Human Services Department, Interior Department, Federal Aviation Administration and Homeland Security Department

Major contracts/projects: General Dynamics Advanced Information Systems won a Navy contract worth $95 million to research, develop and operate information fusion as it relates to the Information Fusion Center established by the Naval Air Warfare Center Weapons Division.

http://www.generaldynamics.com/suppliers/become---a---supplier/

General Dynamics Contact Information:
http://www.gendyn.com/

General Dynamics
2941 Fairview Park
Drive Suite 100
Falls Church, Virginia 22042-4513

Main Number: (703) 876-3000
Fax Number: (703) 876-3125

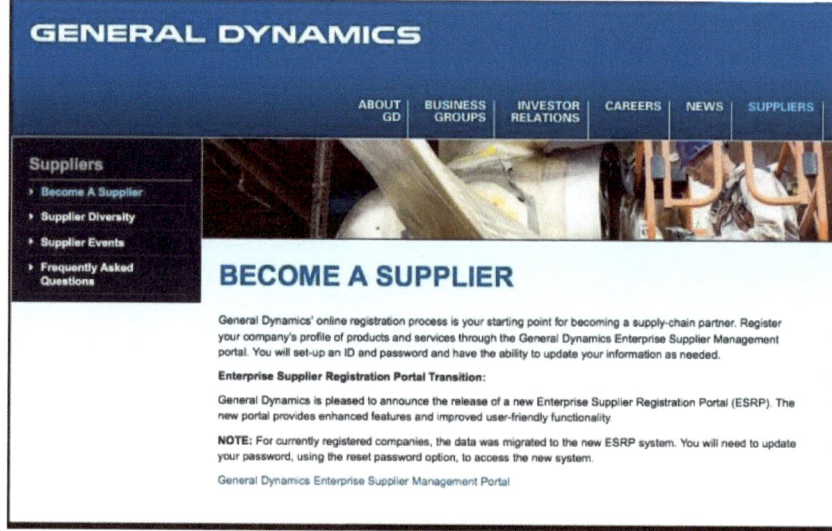

7: Hewlett Packard Co./EDS

Revenue: $4,337,990,000

Headquarters: Palo Alto, Calif.

Web address: http://www.hp.com; http://www.eds.com

President/CEO: Meg Whitman, president and CEO

Head of gov't: Dennis Stokley, senior vice president, U.S. public sector, HP enterprise and services

Ticker: HPQ

Lines of business: Personal systems group, imaging and printing group and enterprise business

Major customers: Homeland Security Department, Treasury Department, Energy Department, Defense Department, Navy, Airforce and Veteran Affairs Department

Major contracts/projects: EDS is the prime contractor for the Navy-Marine Corps Intranet. Under a contract with the Defense Information Systems Agency, the company is providing security readiness reviews for the Defense Department under a $111 million contract.

EDS Is Now HP Enterprise Services

The name change places the global power and recognition of the HP brand behind EDS' technology services portfolio.

HP Enterprise Services Business Information Request:
https://h10134.www1.hp.com/ssl/forms/businessinquiry/index.aspx

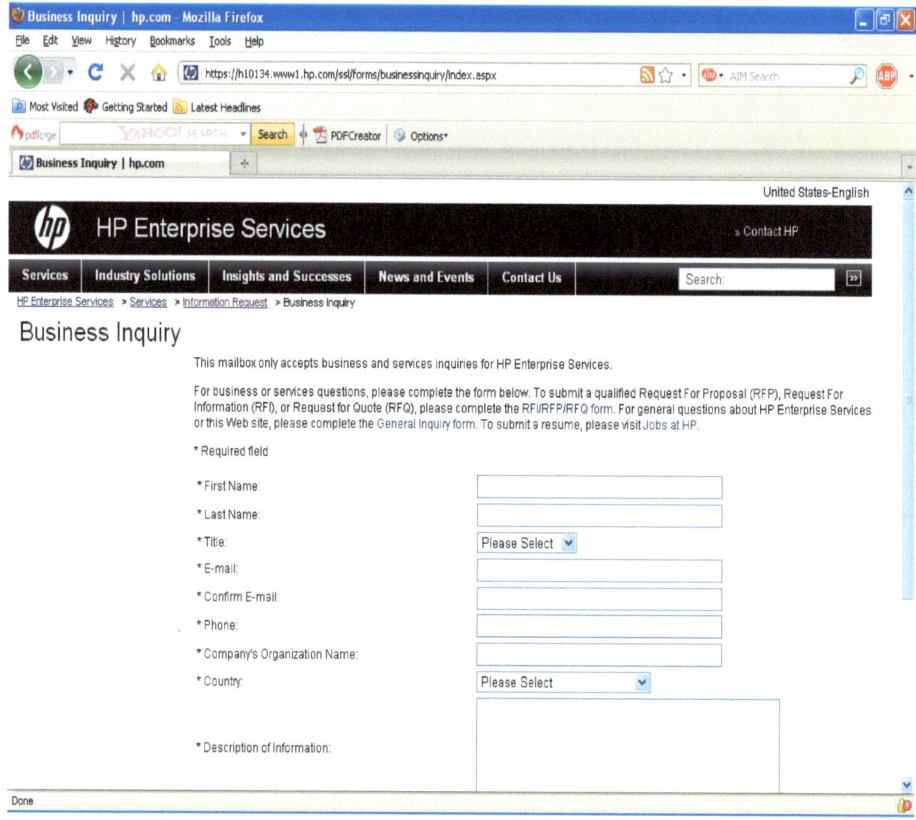

8: Booz Allen Hamilton Inc.

Revenue: $3,946,218,000

Headquarters: McLean, Va.

President/CEO: Ralph W. Shrader

Organization and strategy, economic and business analysis, supply chain and logistics, intelligence and operations analysis, information technology, systems engineering and integration, assurance and resilience and modeling and simulation

Major customers: Defense Department, Air Force, Army, Navy, Marine Corps, Energy Department, Health and Human Services Department, Homeland Security Department, Justice Department, Labor Department, Transportation Department, Treasury Department, NASA, Centers for Disease Control and Prevention, Environmental Protection Agency, General Services Administration and Internal Revenue Service

Major contracts/projects: Booz Allen won a $120 million IT services contract to support the Army Material Command under the Strategic Services Sourcing contract. The company is providing systems engineering and integration services to help transform the Army's enterprise logistics business.

Doing Business with Booz Allen Hamilton

To maintain a competitive advantage, Booz Allen Hamilton teams with best-in-class large and small businesses to complement our services strategy and to offer our clients comprehensive, innovative solutions. Booz Allen also seeks services, products, and technologies from businesses to ensure our firm has a sound infrastructure and the latest technologies to enhance our working environment.

We encourage you to explore our service offerings to learn more about the full range of services the firm offers and our current target industries and markets.

BAH Business Registration Portal:
https://doingbusiness.bah.com/sbp/jsp/index.do?dispatch=viewContent

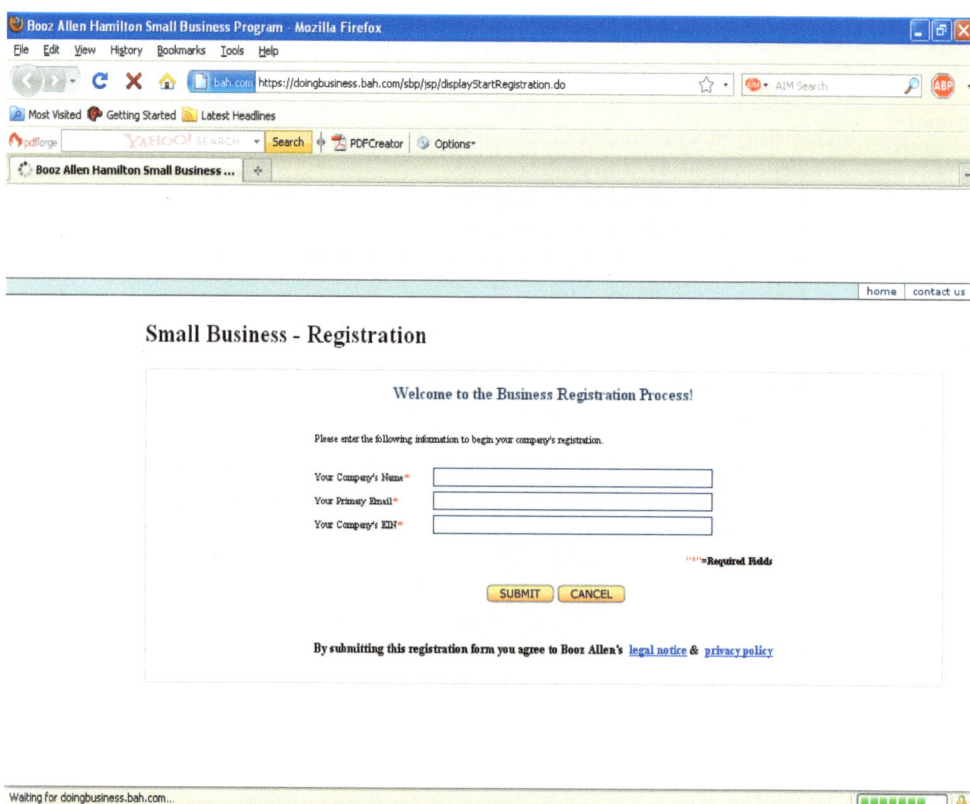

9: Computer Sciences Corp.

Revenue: $3,156,945,000

Headquarters: Falls Church, VA

Web address: http://www.csc.com

President/CEO: Michael Lawrie, chairman, president/CEO

Head of gov't: David Zolet, president North American sector

public Ticker: CSC

Lines of business: Consulting, systems integration and outsourcing

Major customers: Defense Department, NASA, Navy, Army, Air Force, Treasury Department, Health and Human Services Department, Environmental Protection Agency, Transportation Department and State Department

Major contracts/projects: Computer Sciences Corp., was awarded a Software Engineering and Specialized Scientific Support blanket purchase agreement to provide information technology and information management services to the EPA"s Office of Research and Development. The contract is worth $110 million

CSC Supplier Diversity

Suppliers offering products and services for which CSC has requirements are encouraged to enter their information into the CSC Supplier Database by submitting a supplier profile. Confirmation e-mail will be sent once the profile is completed.

Our Supplier Diversity activities frequently receive praise and recognition from U.S. Government agencies. Learn more in our Government Small Business Pages.

| Outreach Events | Supplier Profile |
| Contact Us | Mentor-Protégé Programs |

Related Information
Learn how to work with CSC and find other valuable resources for small businesses.

CSC Supplier Registration:

http://supplier.csc.com/survey.aspx

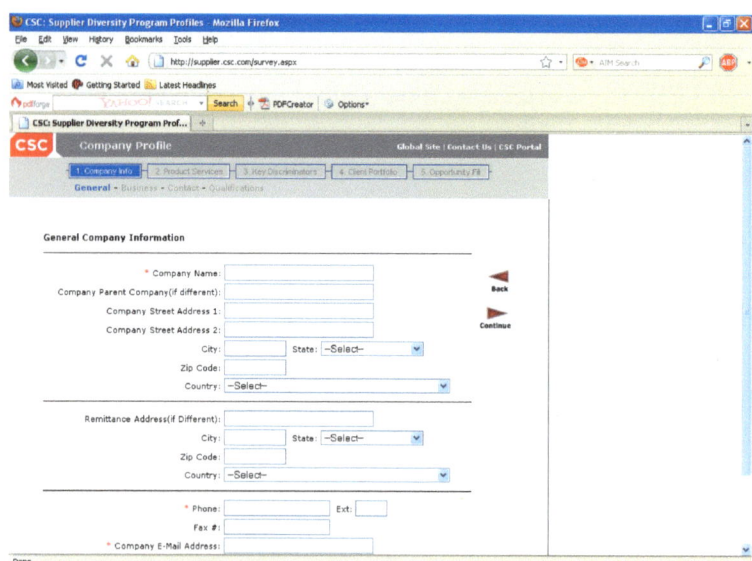

10: L-3 Communications Inc.

Revenue:	$2,535,283,000
Headquarters:	New York City, NY
Web address:	http://www.l-3com.com
President/CEO:	Michael T. Strianese, chairman, president and CEO
Ticker:	LLL
Lines of business:	Command, Control, Communications, Intelligence, Surveillance and Reconnaissance; Government Services; Aircraft Modernization and Maintenance; Electronic Systems
Major customers:	Army, Marine Corps, Navy and Centers for Disease Control & Prevention
Major contracts/projects:	L-3 Communications is providing mine detection systems and accessories to the Army under a 10-year $300 million contract.

SUPPLIER REGISTRATION

Thank you for registering your company on the L-3 Communications Supplier Registration page. This registration is intended to provide L-3 divisions with basic information about your company and your capabilities. Completion of this supplier registration form is no guarantee of continuing or future business with L-3 Communications. Some divisions may require additional information (representations and certifications, quality assurance information, etc) prior to evaluating the potential for doing business with your firm. Further inquiries should be sent directly to the business unit(s) that you have targeted for the marketing of your products or services. Please note that you will not receive a confirmation upon completion of your registration.

L-3 Supplier Registration: http://www.l-3com.com/supplier-info/registration.aspx

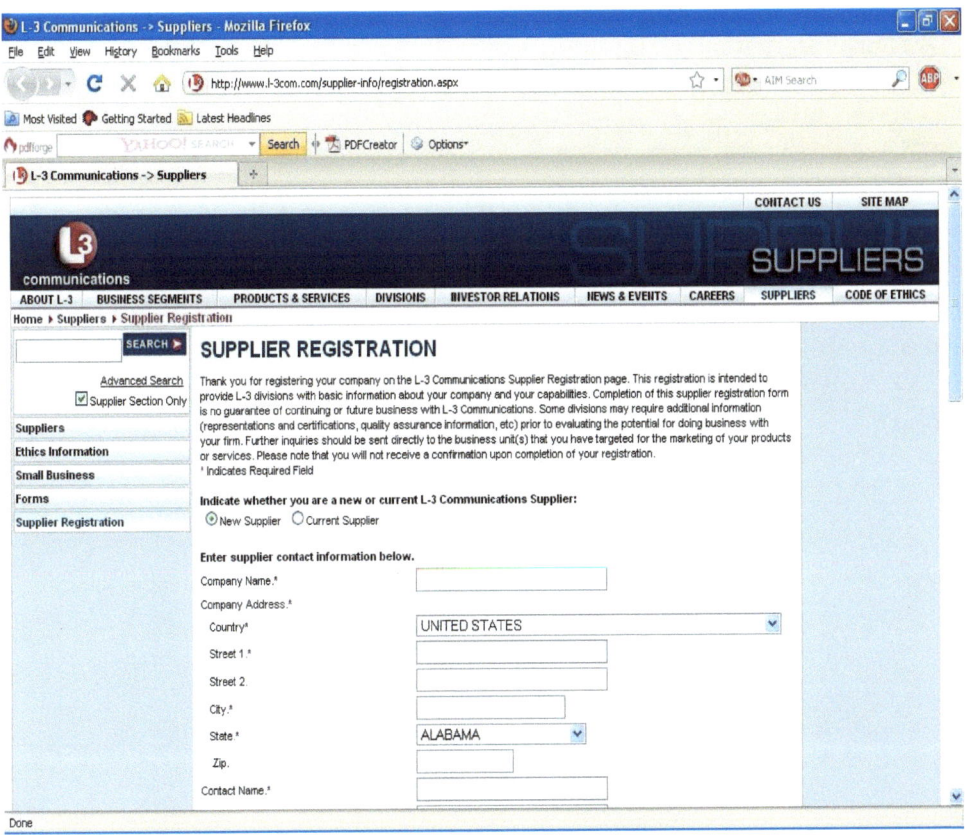

11: DynCorp International LLC

Revenue: $2,263,021,000

Headquarters: Falls Church, Va.

Web address: http://www.dyn-intl.com/

President/CEO: Steven F. Gaffney, chairman and CEO

Head of gov't: Steven T. Schorer, president

Ticker: DCP

Lines of business: Law enforcement training and support, security services, base operations, aviation services, contingency operations and logistics support

Major customers: Defense Department, State Department, Federal Emergency Management Agency and Federal Aviation Administration

The Army hired DynCorp under the $93 million Field and Installation Readiness Support contract to manage the Field Logistics Readiness Center at Fort Bliss, Texas. DynCorp will provide augmentation support to the Army for equipment maintenance, Depot repair, and installation of Modification Work Orders for Automotive Systems, Power Generation Systems, Weapons, Communications Systems, and receipt, storage, and issue of parts, packing and shipping.

SUPPLIERS

Partners in Innovation
DynCorp International is always on the lookout for suppliers who are as innovative and committed to their customers as we are. And we welcome the opportunity to support small and minority-owned businesses. Want to tell us about your company? Please visit our Small Business Database.

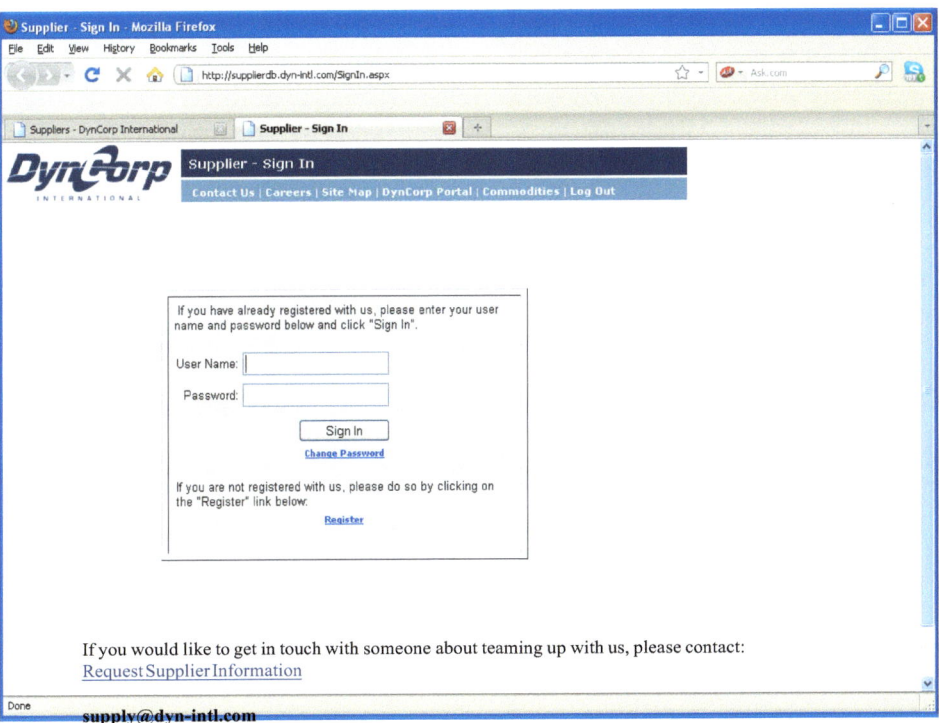

supply@dyn-intl.com

12: CACI International Inc.

Top 100 Revenue: $2,207,441,00

Headquarters: Arlington, Va.

Web address: http://www.caci.com

President/CEO: J.P. London, chairman Head of gov't business: Kenneth Asbury, CEO

Ticker: CAI

Lines of business: Business system solutions, C4ISR integration services, cyber security, information assurance and information operations, data, information and knowledge management, enterprise IT and network services, integrated security and intelligence solutions, logistics and material readiness and program management and SETA support services

Major customers: Navy, Army, Defense Department, State Department, Homeland Security Department, Commerce Department and Defense Information Systems Agency

CACI is providing worldwide logistics support to the Navy's Military Sealift Command under a 10-year contract worth $134 million.

Doing Business with

CACI Follow the steps

1. Review our business solutions and our services and major programs from the **Programs** pull-down menu at the top of each page on this website
2. If you are a small business of any type we urge you to register in the DoD's Central Database SAM.GOV . SAM is a primary search tool used by CACI and others to identify and qualify new small business subcontracting sources.
3. Contact someone listed
   - in our individual business solutions or our **Programs** sections
   - on the Key Contacts page
4. Submit an Information or Contact Request Form

CACI Supplier Information Request:
http://www.caci.com/webapp/grps/contactform.aspx

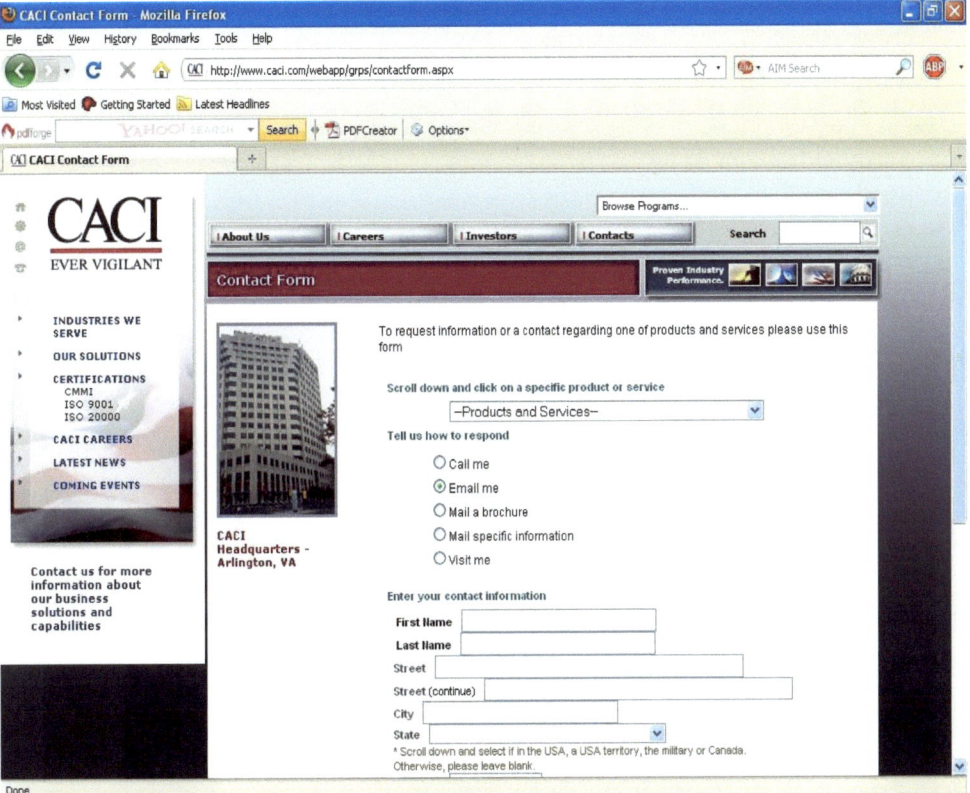

13: Harris Corp.

Revenue: $2,054,146,000
Headquarters: Melbourne, VA.
Web address: http://www.harris.com
President/CEO: William Brown president and CEO
Ticker: HRS

Lines of business:	RF Communications, defense programs, national intelligence programs, civil programs, IT services, broadcast communications
Major customers:	Census Bureau, Federal Aviation Administration, National Reconnaissance Office, Navy, Defense Department and General Services Administration
Major contracts/projects:	Harris Corp. is one of the winners of the multiple-award $50 billion Alliant contract for providing integrated IT solutions to federal agencies. The company also has the Defense Military Health System's global Healthcare Artifact and Image Management Solution (HAIMS) contract.

Becoming a Supplier

We welcome you as a potential supplier to Harris Corporation. This page contains links to supplier qualification information and forms. Please read all of the applicable information carefully and thoroughly before applying for consideration as a potential supplier.

The first links will take you to the Supplier Qualification Forms. It is required that you complete either the Prospective Supplier Qualification or the Small Business Supplier Qualification form in its entirety and submit it to Harris for review. This form has been designed to answer your preliminary inquiries and determine whether or not there is a possibility of a good business fit between our enterprises. We appreciate your cooperation in following our process, and a Harris representative will contact you after your qualification has been reviewed.

Prospective Supplier Form:
http://www.govcomm.harris.com/suppliers/smallbusiness/prospective-supplier-form.asp

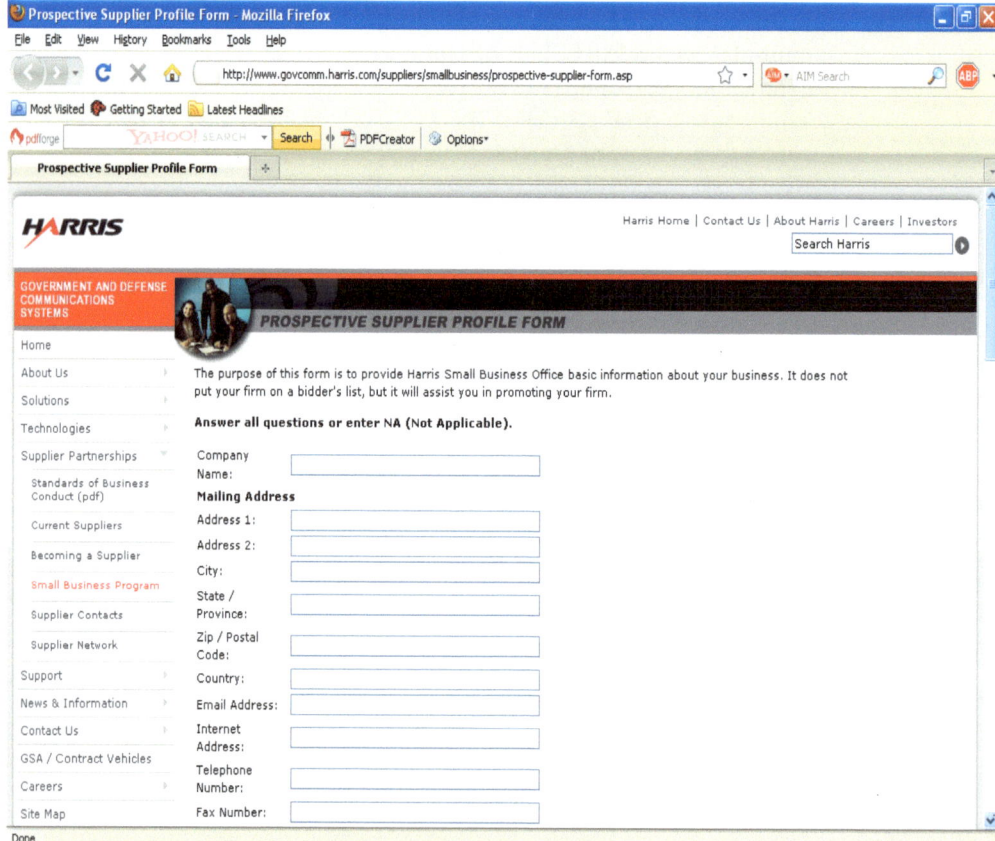

14: Verizon Communications Inc.

Top 100 Revenue:
$2,011,065,000

Headquarters:
New York City, NY

Web address: http://www.verizon.com

President/CEO:
Lowell McAdams, chairman and CEO

Head of gov't
John Stratton, group president, Verizon Federal

Ticker: VZ

Lines of business: Residential, business and wireless

Major customers: General Services Administration, Defense Department, Army and NASA

Major contracts/projects: Verizon Business is providing information technology solutions and professional services to federal agencies under a 10-year General Services Administration contract. The contract has a total value of $50 billion.

Supplier Community

Suppliers are critical to the success of our business and the customers we support. Verizon relies on its suppliers to provide the products and services we need to deliver high growth communications services to our customers when they need them, and at a price they can afford.

Verizon awards business to suppliers based on a competitive procurement process, focusing on continuous improvement in technologies, practices, quality, service and total cost. The Strategic Sourcing Organization manages the acquisition of products and services, and serves as the primary interface to our internal organizations for all supplier interactions.

We have been working and continue to work on evolving our Supplier Interface to be a robust point of entry for current and potential suppliers for online identification, and for access to business critical information. If you are a supplier interested in potential opportunities within Verizon you may register by clicking here. Please see FAQ for questions regarding this process.

You may access key links from our Supplier Interface now. If you are one of Verizon's suppliers currently registered to this site, you may click on Sign In to access your supplier applications, or if you are new to this site, you may click on Register to request access to available applications.

Verizon Supplier Portal:
https://www22.verizon.com/suppliers/registerservlet?action=Registration&actiontype=2

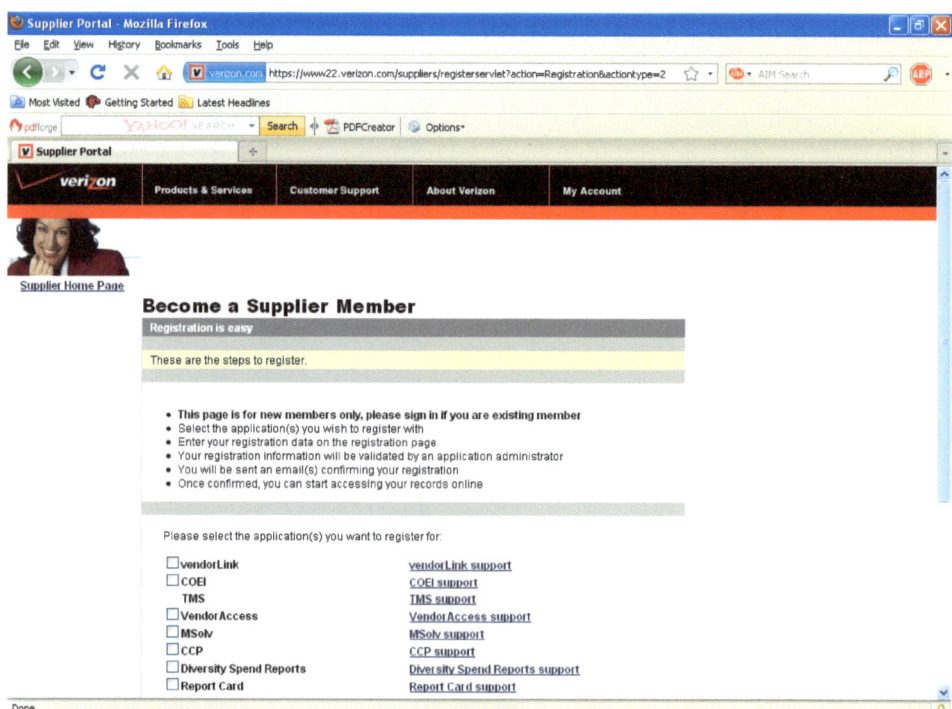

15: ManTech International Corp.

Revenue: $1,947,779,000

Headquarters: Fairfax, Va.

Web address:	http://www.mantech.com
President/CEO:	George J. Pedersen, chairman, CEO and co-founder
Ticker:	MANT
Lines of business:	Defense systems group, information systems and Technology, security and mission assurance and MSRS
Major customers:	Defense Intelligence Agency, Federal Bureau of Investigation, National Geospatial-Intelligence Agency, Homeland Security Department, Navy, Air Force, Justice Department, State Department and NASA
Major contracts/projects:	ManTech won an Army contract worth up to $355 million in February 2009 to provide rapid repair and sustainment of mine-resistant, ambush- protected vehicles.

Supplier Outreach

ManTech recognizes the importance of a comprehensive supplier diversity program and how it impacts the business community.

Our goal is to reach out to the small business community and foster relationships with as many capable, qualified small businesses as possible.

Entrepreneurship and the broadest possible use of specially designated small businesses is essential not only to meeting the demands of Congress and the regulatory code, but also to building growth and forging productive partnerships that are best equipped to meet the needs of our federal government customers. Making the best use of diverse partners in IT and other areas is not only good for society, it's good for business.

ManTech Supplier Registration:
http://www.mantech.com/sb/sb.aspx

16: Fluor Corp.

Revenue: $1,935,182,000

Web address: http://www.fluor.com

President/CEO: David T Seaton, chairman and CEO

Head of gov't business: Bruce A. Stanski, group president, government

Ticker:	FLR
Lines of business:	Energy and chemicals, industrial and infrastructure, government, power and global services
Major customers:	Defense Department, Energy Department, Homeland Security Department, State Department and Labor Department
Major contracts/projects:	Fluor Corp., was hired by the Army to provide support and services to U.S. military and government personnel in the wake of the January 12 Haiti earthquake. Under the Army's Logistics Civil Augmentation Program IV contract, Fluor is building and maintaining several logistical support areas in the general Port-au-Prince vicinity. Fluor is also providing construction services, followed by sustainment services and logistics support.

Suppliers

Fluor's online registration system SCORE!^{SM} provides an easy way for contractors and suppliers to register online. As a global company, Fluor operates across highly diverse markets best served by correspondingly diverse resources, including contractors and suppliers. Fluor is committed to achieving excellence in supplier and contractor diversity throughout its businesses.

Fluor invites companies to register online via its Suppliers and Contractor Online Registry E-version (**SCORE!**^{SM}). Companies may use this tool to indicate that they are a certified diversity supplier or contractor (minority-owned business, women-owned business, small business, small disadvantaged business, HUBZone business, veteran- owned business, and service-disabled veteran-owned business) and follow instructions to attach their certification.

*Recommended Browser is IE 5 or above

http://www.fluor.com/services/procurement/score/Pages/default.aspx

Supplier Registration https://cvmas05.cvmsolutions.com/fluor/New

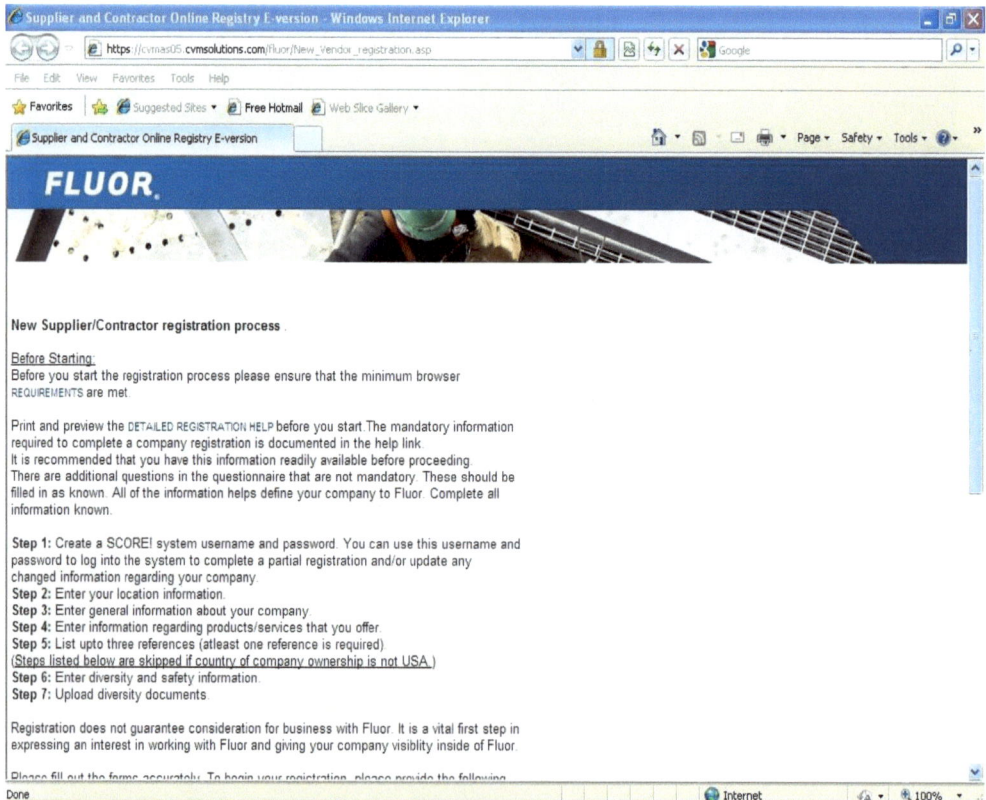

17: AT&T Inc.

Revenue: $1,646,00,000

Headquarters: Dallas, TX

Web address: http://www.att.com

President/CEO: Randall L. Stephenson, chairman and CEO

Head of gov't business: Thomas Harvy, senior vice president, AT&T Government Solutions

Ticker: ATT

Lines of business: Government Solutions, wireless, advanced TV, Internet and DSL and home phone

Major customers: Air Force, U.S. Customs & Border Protection, U.S. Postal Service, Marine Corps, Treasury Department, Army, General Services Administration, Defense Information Systems Agency, Internal Revenue Service, Centers for Disease Control and Prevention and Justice Department

Major contracts/projects: AT&T is one of the prime contractors on the Networx telecommunications contract. AT&T Government Solutions also is providing software engineering services for software verification and validation of U.S. Postal Service automated mail-processing and sorting systems under a $20 million contract.

Supplier Information

The prospective supplier registration is an easy process, intended for use by suppliers seeking to do business with the new AT&T. Please note that registration to our database does not imply a contract, or an intent to purchase by AT&T.

NOTE:

- Prospective Suppliers fill out on line registration form.

- Prospective Suppliers Data made available to AT&T Sourcing managers. Please note, Suppliers will only be contacted if additional information is required about the company product or service.

- AT&T sends annual reminder to supplier contacts requesting an update to their profile information. If company profile is not updated, supplier profile will expire from the AT&T database.

AT&T Supplier Registration:
http://www.attsuppliers.com/prospectivereg.asp

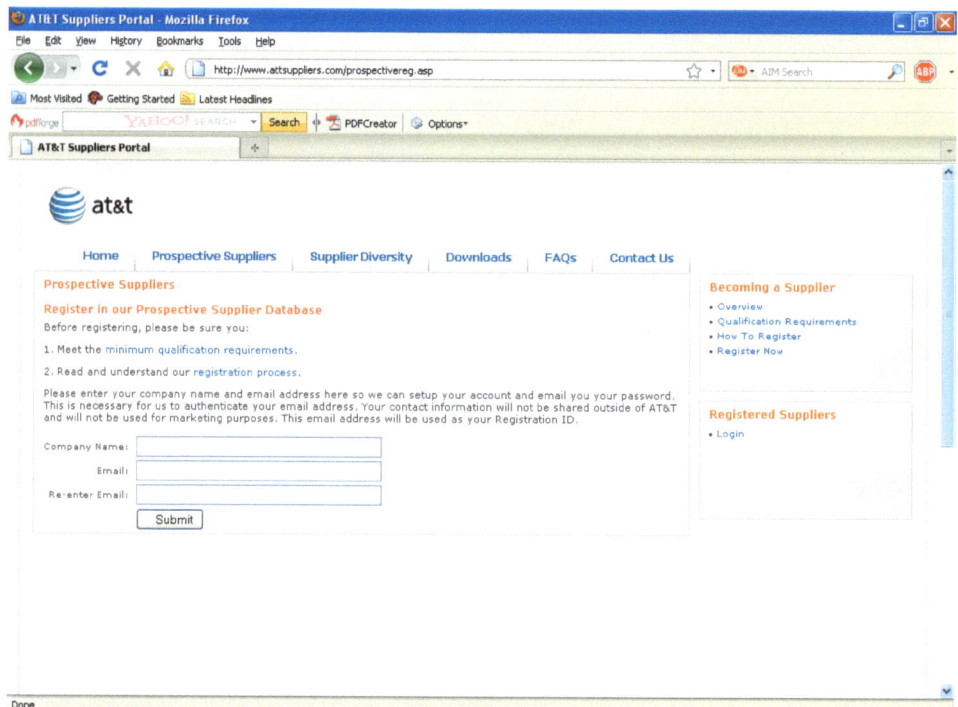

39

18: BAE Systems

Revenue: $1,643,080,000
Headquarters: Rockville, Md.

Web address:	http://www.baesystems.com
President/CEO:	Ian King, chief executive, BAE systems PLC
	Linda Hudson, president and CEO, BAE systems Inc.
Head of gov't business:	
Ticker:	BAESY
Lines of business:	Electronics, intelligence and support, land and armaments, programmes and support and international
Major customers:	Army, Navy, Air Force, Marine Corps, Defense Advanced Research Projects Agency, Treasury Department and NASA
Major contracts/projects:	BAE Systems has an indefinite-delivery/indefinite- quantity contract for federal IT work including infrastructure, applications and IT management services under the new Alliant program.

Suppliers

At BAE Systems we recognize that our ability to meet our customer's needs and to be the premier global defense company is dependent on the Extended Enterprise of the Supply Chain.

In today's competitive global economy we require agile, reliable, innovative and competitive suppliers. We believe strong and resilient relationships with our suppliers, at every level, are critical for us to succeed in meeting our customers' expectations and to continuously improve as a company.

We strive to conduct our business in a principled manner maintaining the utmost integrity and respect for our supply partners.

We are proud to work with a diverse range of companies both large and small. At BAE Systems increasingly emphasis is placed on open architecture, systems integration and through life capability management. We need suppliers who are flexible and open to adapting the way we interact and work together, to deliver a through life service to our customers.

BAE Supplier Registration:
http://www.baesystems.com/BAEProd/groups/public/@businesses/@landarmaments/doc
uments/bae_publication/bae_pdf_mps_sc_sip_7410_main.pdf

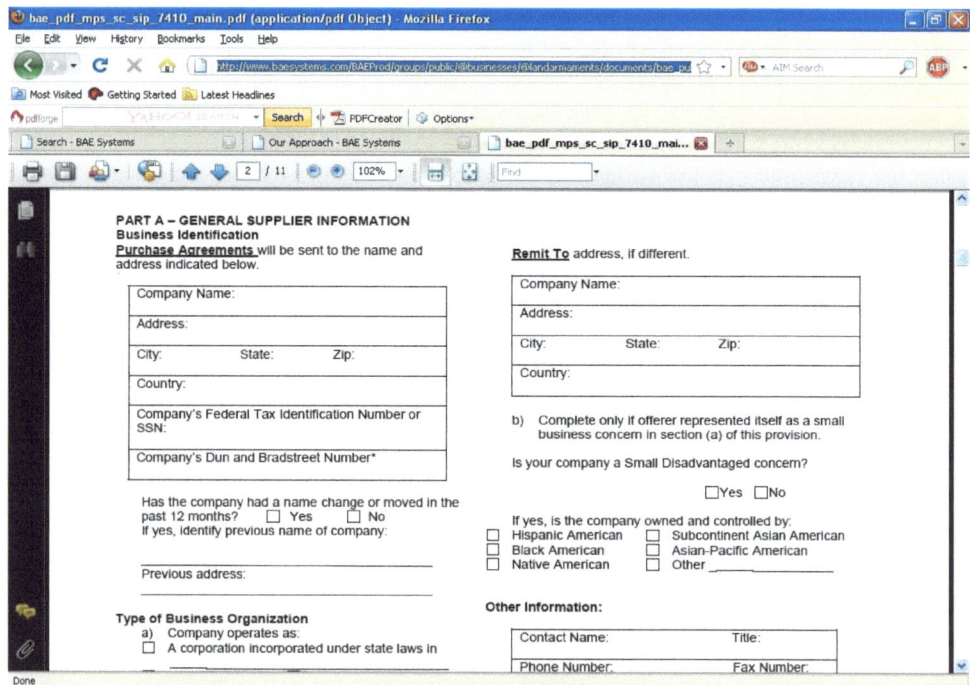

19: Dell Computer Corp.

Revenue: $1,582,009,000

Headquarters:
Round Rock, Texas

Web address: http://www.dell.com

President/CEO: Michael S. Dell, chairman and CEO

Head of gov't business:
Paul D. Bell, president,

Public Ticker: DELL

Lines of business: Home and home office, small and medium business, large business and public sector

Major customers:
Defense Department and other Government Agencies

Major contracts/projects: Dell is providing servers, storage and networking hardware to the Army under the Information Technology Enterprise Solutions - 2 Hardware contract. The contract has a purchasing ceiling of $5 billion.

Suppliers and Diversity

Our online registration is the most widely available method for providing us with information about your business. To be registered in the Dell Supplier Diversity database:

1. Determine whether your company meets the guidelines established by the SBA, NMSDC or WBENC.
2. Complete the Diverse Supplier Profile Form, which provides Dell Supplier Diversity with information about your company.

Please note: Dell Supplier Diversity will review the Profile Form and certification and obtain additional information if necessary. We may not have a current requirement for your capabilities. However, when the need for your product or service does occur, you will be notified and go through our screening process, if your company fully meets our procurement standards.

Dell.com Supplier Registration:
https://ecomm.dell.com/dellstore/myaccount/signup.aspx?c=us&cs=19&l=en&s=dhs

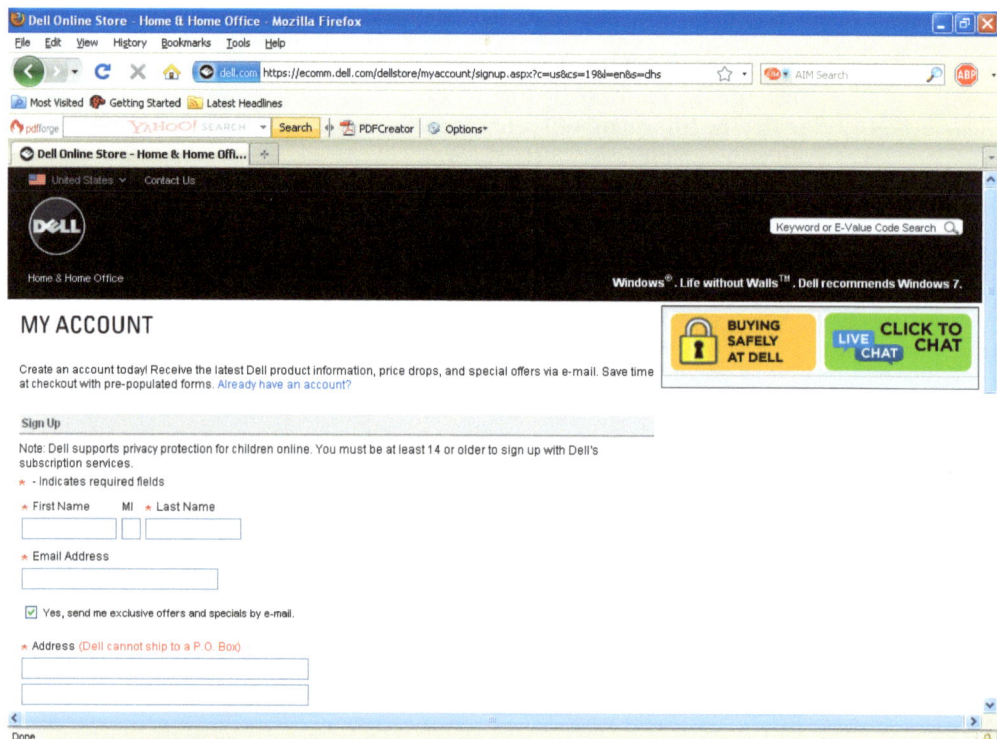

20: United Technologies Corp.

Revenue: $1,567,079,000

Headquarters: Hartford, Conn.

Web address: http://www.utc.com

President/CEO: Louis R. Chenevert, chairman and CEO

Ticker: UTC

Major customers: Carrier, Hamilton Sundstrand, Otis, Pratt & Whitney, Sikorsky, UTC Fire & Security and UTC Power
Energy Department, Navy and Air Force

Major contracts/projects: Pratt & Whitney, a United Technologies company, is providing EcoPower engine wash services for the entire U.S. Air Force F117 fleet of 800 engines, as part of a C-17 F117 Engine Overhaul and Repair support contract from Boeing.

Suppliers

Welcome to the UTC Supplier Registration system. Please take a few minutes to register your business using the form below. You will receive an e-mail confirmation indicating that your information is recorded. We will notify you if there is an opportunity for exploring a business relationship. Registering does not guarantee future business, but does give your company an opportunity for exposure within UTC and its business units.

If you need help with the registration form please contact Technical Support at (713) 439- 0777, or send an e-mail to utc@aecsoftusa.com.

United Technologies Supplier Registration:
http://supplierregistration.utc.com/Supplier/supplier_registration.aspx

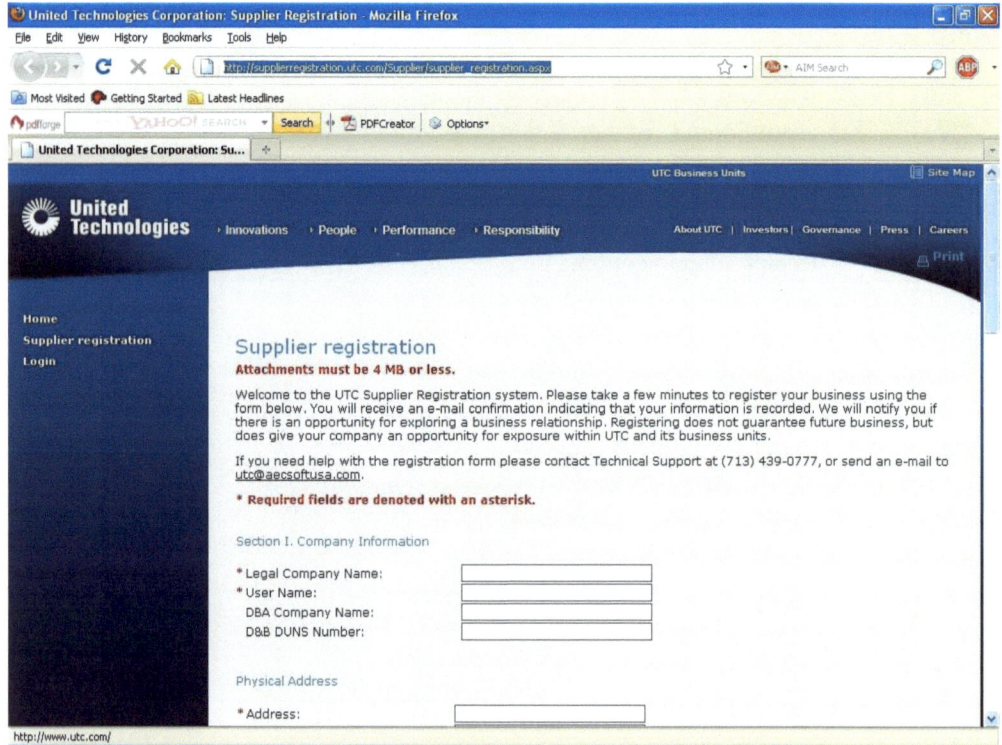

21: IBM Corp.

Revenue: $1,494,073,000

Headquarters:
Armonk, N.Y.

Web address: http://www.ibm.com

President/CEO: Virginia M Rometty, chairman and CEO

Head of gov't
Todd Ramsey, general manager, U.S. federal,I

IBM Ticker: IBM

Lines of business: Small and medium business solutions, business consulting and financing

Major customers: Veterans Affairs Department, Energy Department, Interior Department, Commerce Department and Defense Department

Major contracts/projects: An IBM supercomputer is being used by the Naval Oceanographic Office Major Shared Resource Center to support the oceanographic modeling and analysis needs of researchers at the Defense Department.

Welcome to the Supply Portal

This site is a single entry point for suppliers to access various strategic procurement applications.

- The Public Portal link to the left will lead you to a list of unrestricted procurement applications. **No action** is required to gain access to those applications.
- The My Portal: My Functions link to the left will lead you to a **customized** list of procurement applications and user functions. After clicking on this link, you will be asked for a user ID and password.
    - **First time users:** Register for your user ID and password at the **IBM registration** site. In the future, this will be your single identity for accessing IBM systems over the internet. If you already have an IBM registration user ID and password, you do not have to obtain another.
- Once you have access to 'My Portal: My Functions', the **'User functions'** will allow you to complete administrative tasks, such as requesting access to a specific procurement application or changing your user profile.

IBM Supply Portal: https://www-304.ibm.com/procurement/esi/

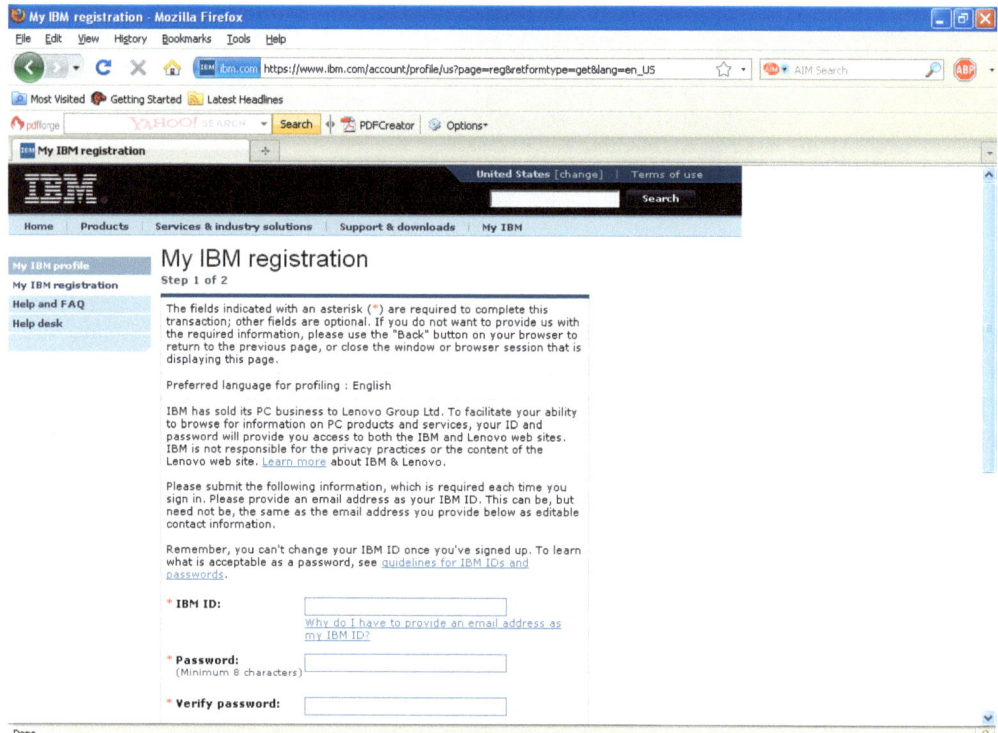

47

22: Exelis (formally ITT)

Revenue: $1,477,317,000
Headquarters: White Plains, N.Y.
President/CEO: David F. Melcher CEO

Lines of business:	Fluid technology, defense electronics and services, motion and flow control
	Marine Corps, Federal Aviation Administration, NASA and Army
Major customers:	Exelis is providing vehicle-mounted systems that Major contracts/projects: prevent the detonation of improvised explosive devices to the Marine Corps. The order is worth

Suppliers

Exelis is a multi-industry organization, but we are committed to doing business with suppliers as one company. Central to our success is the company's Global Strategic Sourcing organization, a globally deployed corporate team of sourcing, transition management and supplier quality professionals.

As current or potential suppliers to Exelis, it is important to know how the organization works, how to integrate into our processes and, in general, to understand the expectations of suppliers engaged with our company. The information contained within this portion of our Web site should provide a good starting point for gaining that understanding.

(Old) ITT Aerospace Supplier Registration:
http://www.ittaerospace.com/supplier_login.asp

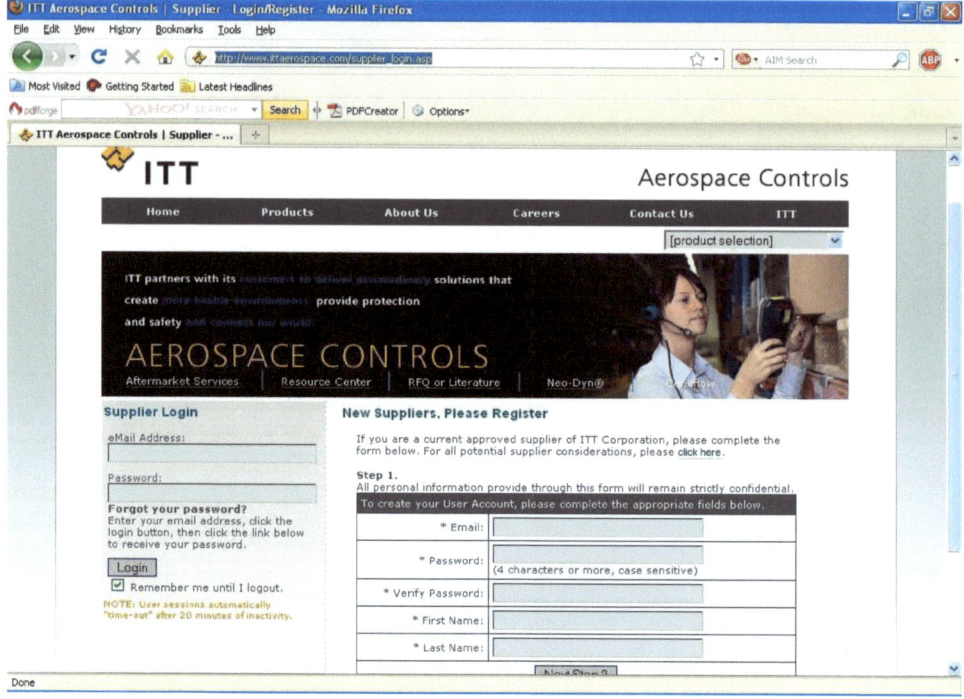

Supplier Diversity

Registration

SUPPLIER REGISTRATION: US BASED COMPANIES

Exelis welcomes inquiries from small businesses. The completion of the form below is the first step in establishing your company as a potential supplier. Your company information will be stored in a central database accessed by all Exelis business units. If there is a requirement for products or services, you will be contacted directly by the interested Exelis business unit.

- Company Name:
- Company Address:
- City:
- State:
- ZIP Code:
- Telephone:
- Fax:
- Email:
- Company Web Site:
- Quality: ☐ AS9100 ☐ ISO 9000 Series
- Point of Contact:
- Year Business Started:
- Number of Employees:
- U.S. Government Security Clearance: None
- Business Type:
- Registered with the Department of State? ○ Yes ◉ No
- Registered to CCR? ○ Yes ◉ No
- DUNS Number:
- Cage Code:
- VAT Code:
- UNSPSC Code (Primary):

Links:

- Central Contracting Registry
- Department of Defense Small Business Programs
- Federal Acquisition Jumpstation
- Federal Aviation Administration
- NASA Small Business
- U.S. Army Small Business Programs
- U.S. Small Business Administration
- UNSPSC Home Page
- U.S. Dept. of Veteran Affairs
- National Minority Supplier Development Council (NMSDC)
- Women's Business Enterprise National Council (WBENC)
- Diversity Inc.com

NAICS Code (Primary):	[ ]
Alternative commodity, product, or service definition (Primary):	[ ]
Other Code (define below):	[ ]
Define Other Code:	[ ]
Identify your Diverse Business Classification as defined by the U.S. Small Business Administration:	☐ Small Owned ☐ Woman Owned ☐ Disadvantaged Owned ☐ Veteran Owned ☐ Service Disabled Veteran Owned ☐ 8(a) Owned ☐ HUBZone Owned
Current Exelis Corporate supplier? (Have an established/active Corporate Supply Agreement)	○ Yes ● No
Current Exelis Business Unit supplier? (Please identify ITT Exelis Business Unit below)	○ Yes ● No
Exelis Businesses Currently Supplied:	☐ Exelis Business Units Electronic Systems Geospatial Systems Information Systems Mission Systems
Exelis Business Contact Name:	[ ]
Exelis Supplier Code (As indicated on your Exelis Purchase Order, remittance details, payment notice, or check stub):	[ ]

[Submit Profile Application]

23: Jacobs Engineering Group Inc.

Revenue: $1,434,759,000

Headquarters:
Pasadena, Calif.

Web address: http://www.jacobs.com

President/CEO:
Craig L. Martin, president and CEO

Ticker: JEC

Lines of Business: Aerospace and defense, automotive and industrial, buildings, chemicals and polymers, consumer and forest products, energy, environmental programs, Infrastructure, oil and gas, pharmaceuticals and biotechnology, refining and technology

Major customers: Defense Information Systems Agency, Army and Air Force

Jacobs, one of 14 companies on the agency's ENCORE II Information Technology Solutions contract, is providing net-centric solutions, including network engineering, analysis and support to various agencies under this $12.2 billion deal.

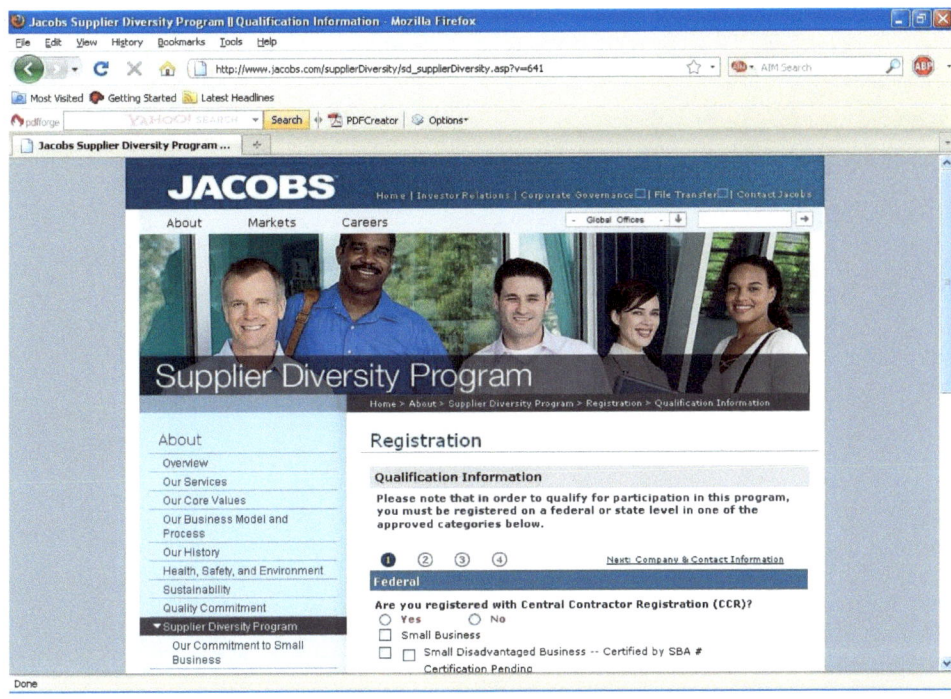

24: Deloitte

Revenue: $1,260,481,000

Headquarters: New York City, NY

Web address: http://www.deloitte.com

President/CEO: Joe Echevarria

Head of gov't business: Robin Lineberger, principal, Deloitte Consulting LLP and leader, Deloitte Federal government services

Lines of business: Consulting: technology integration, strategy and operations, human capital, enterprise applications, outsourcing; Financial Advisory Services: business intelligence services, analytics and forensics, capital projects consulting, reorganization services; Audit and Enterprise Risk Services: internal audit, security and privacy services, risk intelligence, control assurance; Tax: tax advisory services

Major customers: Defense of Department, Navy, Defense Information Systems Agency, Department of Homeland Security, Transportation Security Administration, Immigration and Customs Enforcement, Department of Justice, Internal Revenue Service, Department of Health and Human Services, Social Security Administration, Department of Agriculture, Department of Education and Department of Interior

Major contracts/projects:

Deloitte Contact Information:
https://www.deloitte.com/view/en_US/us/Contact-us/Email-Us/index.htm

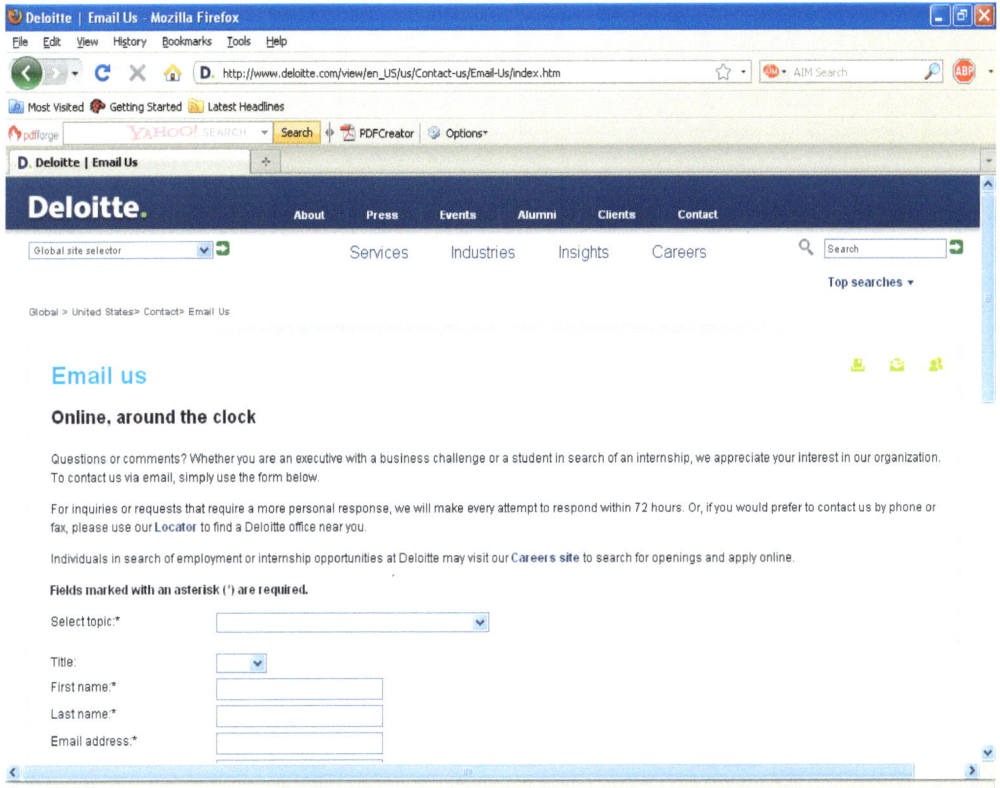

25: Accenture Ltd

Revenue: $1,200,398,000

Headquarters: Dublin, Ireland

Web address: http://www.accenture.com

President/CEO: Pierre Nanterme, CEO

Head of gov't: Kay Kapoor

Ticker: ACN

Lines of business: Communications and high tech, financial services, products, resources and public service

Major customers: Homeland Security Department, Air Force and Army

Major contracts/projects: The Federal Emergency Management Agency hired Accenture to provide program management and business architecture services for the agency's flood risk mapping, assessment and planning program.
The contract is worth $58 million.

Accenture Supplier Registration:

Suppliers

Suppliers interested in doing business in the United States or globally, including the United States:

If you are interested in offering a product or service to Accenture, please go to the Supplier Portal to create a user account and a profile with information about your company and the services or products you offer. Your information will be entered into Accenture's database for future consideration. If there are any opportunities in which your company fits, you will be contacted. Registered suppliers can visit the Supplier Portal at any time to update their company profile.

Please note that Accenture has both a preferred supplier program and a supplier diversity program in place. Only those suppliers registered via this process will be considered for these programs.

Accenture Supplier Registration:

https://cvmas11.cvmsolutions.com/accenture/new_vendor_registration.asp (Compatible with Internet Explorer)

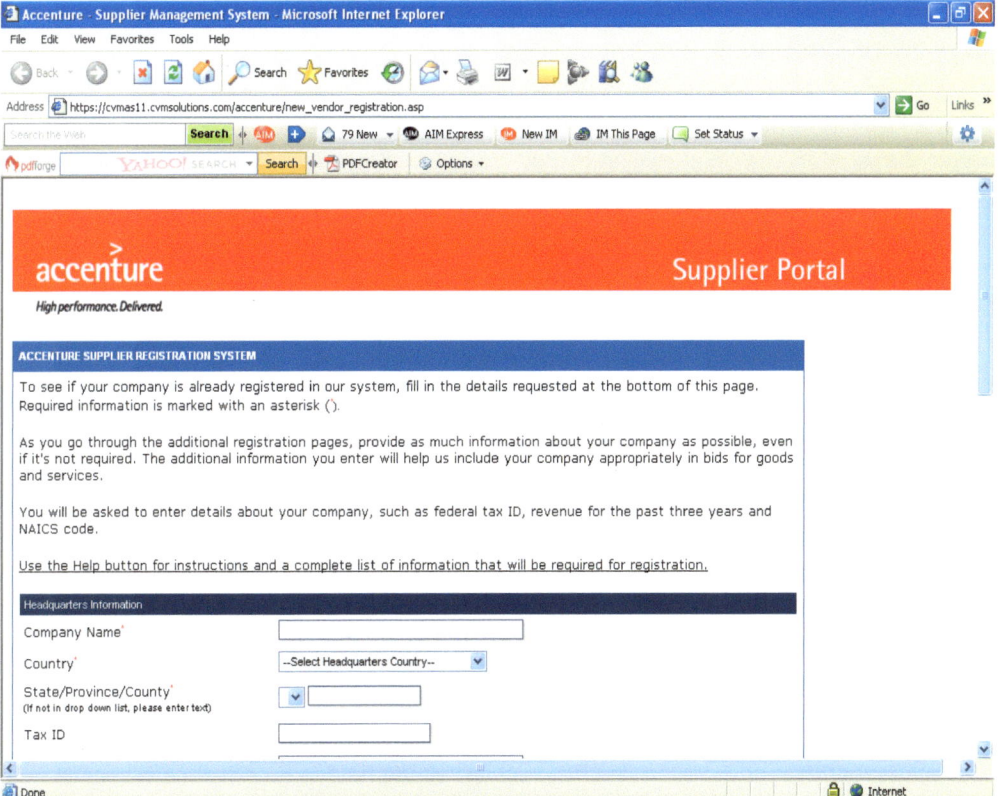

Thank You for Purchasing :

The Billionaires Club: The Top 25 Federal Contractors

If you have any questions please email me at:

info@whetzelgroup.com

Howard C. Whetzel

www.ingramcontent.com/pod-product-compliance
Lightning Source LLC
Chambersburg PA
CBHW040847180526
45159CB00001B/340